The Four Foundational Questions of Faith

Editorial Content: AnnaMarie McHargue
Design: Leslie Hertling

Printed in the United States of America
ISBN: 978-1-7334151-1-8

Table of Contents

Foreword

Questions define your life. The quality of your life may well be determined by the caliber of your questions. Ask the wrong questions and you will obtain the wrong answers. Ask shallow questions and you may develop a shallow life. Ask no questions and your life is likely to be captivated by whatever circumstance you stumble into next. Choose your questions well!

Life, by its nature, generates a multiplicity of questions. As soon as newborn babies gain a sense of awareness of their surroundings, primitive thoughts begin forming in their minds. Who is that person who is feeding me? Who is that creature making those strange sounds and sticking his smiling face into mine? As we grow older, our questions become more defined, and harder to answer.

There are perhaps a handful of questions—and their corresponding answers—that lay the foundation to our life. Who am I? Why am I? Where did I come from? Do I have a purpose? How do I measure my success? How do I live intentionally? Joyfully? Is there a God? If there is a God, why does He allow evil and suffering to afflict people? What, if anything, lies on the other side of death? Am I ready to die? Some people wrestle with these questions throughout their existence. Others blissfully ignore them, hoping things will just work out on their own. Still others have a nagging sense that there must be more to their existence than what meets their eye, yet they are unwilling or too busy to take the time to seek answers for their dis-ease. Sadly, some people wait until the end of their life to consider the purpose of their existence. Worse yet, some people live their entire lives without considering whether they had any greater purpose than paying off their mortgage and getting their children through college. Life is far too important and precious to spend carelessly or thoughtlessly!

Thirteen years ago I began working closely with CEOs of some of America's largest companies. I had worked with pastors and seminary professors for many years and thought that would always be my life's focus. But I soon discovered that working with these top level, successful businesspeople also brought me great delight. That's because they are supremely pragmatic. They are not ivory tower theorists. They want solid answers that work and stand the test of time. They don't play games. They don't waste time. They are intolerant of careless work or sloppy thinking. They expect value for their effort and investment.

It was while working with these CEOs that I first met Scott MacLellan. Scott fits the profile of a highly successful business leader. He is bright, great with people, and accustomed to success. He has initiated highly successful startups. He is currently the CEO of a billion-dollar company. He leads thousands of staff. He solves significant problems every week. A mistake could cost his company millions of dollars, so Scott rarely makes them. As a result, Scott is accustomed to solving problems and finding answers to his questions. That's why I'm so excited about Scott MacLellan's new book, *Am I. The Four Foundational Questions of Faith.* In his book, Scott takes the same pragmatic, thoughtful, inquisitive approach that has made him so successful in business and uses it to find answers to life's most vexing questions. Scott isn't distracted by secondary matters. He focuses on root issues. It is in concentrating his considerable analytical powers upon life's most important questions that Scott is at his best. He systematically works through the issues that matter most to ordinary people.

However, if you presume that, due to his executive level lifestyle, he has never experienced the pain and frustration experienced by the average person, you would be mistaken. Scott and his sweet wife Deborah have endured heart-wrenching pain and disappointment over the course of their marriage. They have had doctors inform them that their precious little daughter's illness was most likely terminal. They have battled that same child's long-term addiction due to prescription pain meds. They have spent sleepless nights concerned for a missing child. They have received the late-night phone calls that is every parent's nightmare. Scott's questions are not pursued in a disinterested, casual manner. He has experienced some of the best and some of the worst that life has to offer, and that has inspired him to find answers that make sense of it all. You will find Scott to be humble, candid, and transparent about his own struggles, fears, frustrations, and pain. Scott does not write as an expert who boasts of his flawless experiences and successes. Rather, he writes as a businessperson, a spouse, a parent, a vulnerable creature of dust, who is trying to make sense of the complications of life. It won't take you long to identify with him as a fellow pilgrim in search of answers.

As you read this book, begin by praying that your heart and mind would be receptive to the truth you will encounter on its pages. You may want to identify the questions you have for God, and for yourself. The pages you read will undoubtedly raise questions and insights you have never considered before. You might experience a major spiritual breakthrough. You might become disturbed, or even angry. That's okay. No one said finding answers to humanity's most pressing problems was going to be easy. But at the end of the day, you will have bravely faced life's most compelling questions and done so in the company of a winsome, candid, honest fellow traveler searching for the same answers as you. I pray that, as you read the following pages, you will discover all that you need to experience a joyful, meaningful, and abundant life and faith.

—Dr. Richard Blackaby,
President of Blackaby Ministries International,
international speaker, and author and co-author
of over 35 books, including *Experiencing God*.

Christianity, if false, is of no importance, and if true, of infinite importance. The only thing it cannot be is moderately important.

—*C. S. Lewis*

Faith and Belief

If there is a crisis of belief in today's world, it is not what we may think. The crisis is not that we have stopped truly believing, it's that we no longer know what belief actually is. Faith and belief are relegated to our holy books, based on stories that happened a long time ago. We may revere the book, but never read it. We may believe strongly in our religion, or be convinced of our own spirituality, but never really understand what our religion stands for or what spirituality even means.

As a result, we tend to believe in generalities, in things and people who sit outside our daily lives, governing from on high in a place far, far away. But faith is found in the specifics of our daily lives, in the messy details of what happens to each of us every day. These details assail us continuously over the years, as we compare the idea of what our lives should be like with what our lives actually are—and how God could possibly be involved.

One of my favorite Biblical characters is David. He was a king and "a man after God's own heart." But he was also a mess, and his life was periodically in chaos. Some would argue that he was a brilliant ruler, but he also was an adulterer and a murderer who spent many of his days as a fugitive. David's life was not the utopia I'm sure he envisioned when he was told he would be the next king of Israel.

And yet, outside of Jesus, David had the most intimate relationship with God we see in the Bible. David involved God in every aspect of his life, including his most spectacular triumphs and his most awful tragedies. He claimed none of the credit for the good in his life and took all of the blame for the bad. God, to David, was as real as any other person in his life.

That was belief. That was faith built upon every interaction, every moment of David's specific life. And so, our faith must be built upon the actual experiences we have in our own lives. Your life and my life are different, but they are created lives nonetheless. I am what God designed, and you are what God designed. He has a different purpose for each of us, even while having the same goal of relationship and eternal life.

For decades I have been on a journey to understand and embrace my relationship with God, assuming, of course, there actually is one. My belief, assumptions, and intermittent hope in Him have waxed and waned over the years, especially during times of constant strife and struggle. My life has turned out to be quite different than what I envisioned, not at all the fairy tale we all hope for.

The realities of my own adult life hit hard, and I knew I had to make choices—decisions—about how I would live in the midst of constant crisis and how I would believe in a God who was with me in the midst of it.

The Testing of Our Faith

Whether we profess deep faith or no faith, not many of us truly contemplate what it means to deeply believe whatever it is that we claim to believe. It is not until a crisis that we start genuinely asking questions of faith, and then usually only so long as the crisis lasts.

In my case, our family crisis lasted almost 30 years, and so my questions lingered longer than most. They kept me in a state that would not allow me the indulgence of having no opinion on matters of faith. At some point—or more like at many points—I had to decide that there was a God, or there was not a God. I could no longer camp in middle ground and explain the purpose of my life to myself or to others. With no faith *conviction*, I had only weak platitudes and excuses for a God I wasn't even sure I believed in any more.

I did not have a dark night of the soul; I had dark decades of the soul. Had I only had one night, I would have survived the night, quickly and easily reverting back to a faith of blind indifference, one I even professed strongly at times. I could have survived a year without diving deep into my faith story. Eventually, though, I was forced to take the *concept* of my

Christian faith and either turn it into something real or crucify it. I'd either understand how my faith could practically impact the life I had been given, or I would need to toss it aside and not frustrate myself any longer.

Our family's story is not all that important to the theme of our conversation, but it may add some credibility to the content of this narrative. Our youngest daughter is a three-time cancer survivor, has had two liver transplants and more than 150 surgeries in her lifetime. After her second liver transplant, she grew addicted to pain medication and spent more than a decade dealing with one form of addiction or another. The devastation to our daughter, and also to our family, was severe. It wasn't daily trauma. It was minute-by-minute trauma. It never, ever let go. I could never understand how a good God could allow all that to happen.

With no faith conviction, I had only weak platitudes and excuses for a God I wasn't even sure I believed in any more.

That was my crisis of faith, and I'm sure you've had yours. We all have our own stories. In the end, for me, the suffering was necessary to force me to understand who I was and what I believed. Without it, I would still be living a myth, a story, and a concept of faith that had no real meaning or application to me or anyone else around me. I would still be professing a faith that I didn't completely understand or trust in.

Oswald Chambers, a renowned teacher, once said that a position is not your own until you claim it through suffering. I can now fully claim my position, but it's been a long road, and my faith was put through the press. I am grateful to have emerged after my trials assured that God *is*, that He is *great* (in control), and that He is *good*.

For those of us familiar with the content of the Bible, that which we believe to be God's Word, we know God to be Yahweh, the great I Am. "I Am" is a declarative statement and not a question. And yet I believe that in God's wonderful mercy and grace, He is willing to be vulnerable and transform His statement into a question: "Am I?" The question seems so simple, so elementary, but it is profound in its impact to our faith walk. It's the first, and most important, question we must answer.

Most people would answer, "Of course, there is a God" or "Of course, there isn't." And yet I would propose that the vast majority of people in actuality sit somewhere between these two responses no matter how they answer that question. We are a people of the middle ground. Most people don't actually know what they believe when it comes to matters of faith. They may have strong opinions, but not a deeply held conviction when pressed.

He is willing to be vulnerable and transform His statement into a question: "Am I?"

I confess that I still spend a great deal of time contemplating my answer to this all-important question. Ironically, I don't struggle with other questions that assume there is a God. I know that God loves me, is for me, and is integrated into every aspect of my life, even my pain. I know He is all-powerful, all-knowing, wise, and the creator of my very being. I believe He is an awesome God, but still I struggle with unbelief.

I have come to suppose that beliefs must be questioned and tested to grow into faith. Otherwise they are just beliefs, easily held with no substance at a critical moment of choice. Faith must be tested, or it is not faith at all. Untested faith is theory, supposition, and presumption.

I would imagine that the father who cried out to Jesus to heal his son in Mark, Chapter 9, believed in many things. But when asked if he believed that Jesus could heal his child specifically, right in that moment, he had to declare what he knew deep in his soul. Immediately, confusion welled up inside him, and he pleaded for Jesus Himself to come to his aid in providing the most crucial building block to the healing process—the man's own belief system.

But when the man's son was healed, he no longer had to believe. He had seen it with his own eyes. He could feel it in his child's touch. And thus, his belief evolved into something much stronger—conviction. He would spend the rest of his days remembering that moment, having the full knowledge, a knowing, that the Son of God would deliver him when he needed it most. A tested belief became assurance, became knowing, became faith.

Faith must be tested, or it is not faith at all.

You believe first, and your faith follows. But you must be willing to carry your beliefs into difficult terrain, to emerge stronger and more assured. And somewhere deep in the struggle, your Creator and Lord will whisper in your ear a question that invites you to make a choice and leave the safety of your middle ground. "Am I?"

The State of Our Faith

One of the fastest growing segments of religious affiliation, now almost a quarter of the population, is called "Nones" (pronounced nuns); that is, people who have no religious or spiritual belief system. These are not necessarily atheists so much as agnostics. They aren't anti-God, and they may even have some interest in a generic spirituality, but they don't particularly see the importance of the subject.

An argument is made by some data scientists that this crowd is not actually growing in number, but instead finally coming out of the closet. Their claim is that it is more socially acceptable for people to say they have no religious belief system, which gives them permission to admit openly what they have felt all along. The data, therefore, may be giving the false impression that some religions are in decline, while agnosticism is on the rise. Religious belief, perhaps, was never as popular as previously thought in modern analytics.

Regardless, the church today is rightly looking to reach this group of Nones but is stuck in how to do so. If people hold no opinion, or virtually no interest, on matters of faith, it is difficult to engage. Where there is no interest, there is no seeking. Where there is no seeking, there is no listening. Where there is no listening, there is no internal debate or outside viewpoint. With each passing generation, the Nones' perspective becomes increasingly self-oriented. This is not to say they are necessarily selfish; it's just that their entire faith system, or lack thereof, is built on self-perception, or the views of equally indifferent friends.

. . . it is through our own faith that we find a deeper respect and love for people of different faiths.

This may be the greatest faith problem of all. Indifference fails to lead to any kind of religious understanding, either of self or of others. Instead, it is through our own faith that we find a deeper respect and love for people of different faiths. But if we hold no curiosity in the faith question, we lose interest in the most fundamental aspect that defines many cultures. This breeds either neglect or contempt, neither of which holds much hope for a world that claims tolerance as one of its defining characteristics.

How can we be tolerant or respectful of something we do not understand and do not value? We can ignore it, but we cannot respect it. We can pretend it is not there, but we cannot be tolerant of what we do not know. We must know something to actively engage it—to get the most from what that person, or that culture, has to offer. We cannot actively seek that for which we hold no importance, nor can we benefit from something we do not value. I would argue this tolerance our current culture professes is not tolerance at all, but instead a complete lack of interest.

Furthermore, in our society's sincere effort to make others feel welcome and valued, we have diluted our core beliefs or ignored them altogether to make room for other beliefs. This is well intentioned, but faulty thinking. It assumes a zero-sum game, that one group must give up their beliefs in order for the other group to live/express theirs.

The solution is not to dilute our religions, our faith, or our testimonies, but rather to fall more deeply in love with them. People who know what they love and why they love it seek that quality in others. They value strength and commitment and seek to learn how others have found their strength. This is as true for religion as any belief system. Strong, respectful beliefs make for greater tolerance and stronger community, not less.

The solution is not to dilute our religions, our faith, or our testimonies, but rather to fall more deeply in love with them.

For example, I have an enduring friendship with the security guard in my workplace. He is a very faithful Muslim, and I am an enthusiastic Christian. We can talk for long stretches about our faith and never once feel uncomfortable when discussing the other's point of view. That is not to say that our theology is the same, but we both have a deep respect for the other's reverence for God and faith system. I look forward each day to our encounters, and I would venture to say that through our friendship we have more respect both for our own faith, and the other's faith.

The Nones, however, have lost interest in faith and in the process have lost a powerful way to come into community. Perhaps more tragic still is that the category of Nones is larger than any of us realize. I would argue that many of us who call ourselves Christian are more like the Nones than we care to admit. Our faith can be tepid, even while we attend worship or serve our community.

Jesus warned us that not everyone who calls Him *Lord* will enter the kingdom, but only those who do what His Father wills (Matthew 7:21-23). He knew that some of His followers would be followers in name only. He also said that He would prefer that we be hot or cold, not lukewarm (Revelation 3:15-17). He called for us to be bold in one direction or another. And yet, we rarely think about these things, let alone take a position.

It's hard to fall in love with a concept.

Our traditional faith in a specific God has turned into a more universal God, sometimes merely referred to as "the universe." Our belief that God speaks into our lives is either patronized or castigated. Our view of God's supernatural power is relegated to history, if we even believe that His power was ever on display at all. Our belief systems have devolved, becoming powerless and generic. It's no wonder people have lost interest. People fall in love with passionate people and ideas specifically, not generally or mythically. It's hard to fall in love with a concept, and yet that is how many see God in their heart of hearts.

It's easy to see how this devolution happened. It is the path of least resistance. A generic God looks down upon us as a community, with no specific benefit or accountability to us personally. A generic God, an impersonal God, can be explained away and even ignored. There is nothing unique to me and therefore, I can cast my beliefs upon the ups and downs of the community, or leave this God entirely to the myriad of other people who can do my believing for me.

If my belief hinges upon a communal God, or a generic God, my faith cannot be challenged. If I hold no specific belief, no specific expectations, and no specific accountability, there is nothing to be questioned and I can maintain whatever fiction my mind chooses. I am free from controversy, disappointment, and gratitude. Nothing ventured, nothing lost.

But faith is found in the personal details of real people. If my God is personal to me, as well as to my community, then He is *my* God as much as He is *our* God. And if He is my God, then He is God over my life specifically. This means He has expectations of *me* and plans for *me*. If He is my God, then He is a potential cause of the specific bad in my life, and He is to be praised for the specific good.

As important as this realization can be to our long-term faith progression, it is also in this that the crisis of faith hinges. Once hard times hit, we are forced to reconcile our beliefs against the concept of a universal God, or even the faith-specific God we learned about in our childhood—a fiction we have relegated to the background of our previously satisfied lives. But eventually, we learn that concepts cannot explain away our pain, and a gap opens up in our belief system. This is an open door that is as easily walked through as shut behind us.

Our faith is developed by active choice, not by default.

As the generic God we constructed proves incapable of fixing our circumstances, we either go deeper into our understanding of who God really is, or we reject Him altogether. Our previous illusion of the God "out there" allowed us to camp in blissful indifference. This is where we became Nones, maybe not consciously, but in reality.

The God of our life specifically, on the other hand, will either speak to our souls profoundly or disappoint us entirely. It all depends upon what we choose to see, hear, and process deeply. If we wish to live lives of power and grace, we must face this painful moment and survive with some level of belief intact. And then we must do the work required to reconstruct an active and ever-present belief system from the ground up.

Do not allow yourself to remain in the comfort of communal thought, which can mean no thought at all.

Our faith is developed by active choice, not by default. My God and my faith cannot be that of my parents, pastor, or progeny. My faith cannot be dependent upon the faith of my community, the general good, or the general bad. My faith is just that... mine. My faith is unique to my life and all the struggles and blessings that come along with it. If I have it easy, my faith may require of me that I overcome the tendency to think that I could have done all of this on my own. And if I have it rough, then my faith must overcome the thought that God is unlovable at best and cruel at worst.

This journey we must face results from the deliberate actions of a seeker, not as one who is saved but only by escaping through difficult circumstance (1 Corinthians 3:15). We must actively seek, and we must wait on God, which is to say that we anticipate response, we hope for response, and we expect response in due time. His promise is that if we seek, we will find. If we knock, He will answer. If we ask, we will receive (Matthew 7:7).

With that in mind, as you contemplate the text that follows, come strongly into your belief system, whatever that may be. Do not allow yourself to remain in the comfort of communal thought, which can mean no thought at all. Reach out to a God that desires a relationship with you specifically, not at the exclusion of anyone else, but rather to connect you with everyone else.

The questions and thoughts that follow are intended to be a dialogue between you and a personal God. Come as you are, but come!

The Four Foundational Questions of Faith

The Four Questions

Before any of us can progress deeply into our faith journey, there are four key questions we must ask and answer.

1. Does God exist?
2. Who is our God?
3. Is God love?
4. Is God the King of all?

While these questions may seem very simple, they are also profound. Like the Nones, so many believers rest comfortably in saying they are from this religion or that. And yet, most of us cannot truly answer these questions honestly or deeply, either about our communal religion or our personal spiritual selves. Our answers can, at times, tend to be superficial, lazy, and hypocritical. We say one thing, but our actions show that we believe another.

While you could answer these four questions as I have them written above, I would encourage you to answer them instead as if you were in direct conversation with God Himself (or Herself as your belief system may be). It can be easier to dismiss the question if you are answering it intellectually. It is altogether more difficult to realize you are answering a God who knows everything you are thinking already anyway.

So, let me encourage you to ask each question in prayer, in silence, in contemplation. Take your time. You might spend hours, or even weeks getting to the deepest part of your belief system for each one of the four questions. Ask them as if God were in direct dialogue with you. Do not answer as you think you should. Rather, answer as you really feel, and perhaps as you heard from God in the quiet of your meditation.

1. Am I?
2. Who am I?
3. Am I love?
4. Am I the King of all?

Perhaps if it helps in your study, you could also think of your questions with a bit more detail.

1. Am I? Do I even exist? Am I real?
2. Who am I? Am I Jesus? Am I Muhammad? Am I an old white man with a long grey beard? Am I a body or a spirit? Am I a man or woman, or both? What's my name? Where do I live?
3. Am I love? Am I good? Am I for you, against you, or neutral?
4. Am I King of all? Am I in control of the universe, or am I sitting at a distance waiting for you to figure things out? Am I in control of your life, or are you in control of your life? Do you act like I'm in control of your life, or more like you are in control?

To think of how these things come together, you could visualize it like building a pyramid, something designed to last through millennia.

Before we can explore faith in God, we first have to know if we believe in God at all. God either exists, or He doesn't. There is no in between. We can argue what God is like later. But there is either something greater than ourselves, or we are all there is. And so, we must answer the question, "Am I?"

The second question, "Who am I?" is a tough one. Who is it that we are praying to? This is the fundamental question of most religions. Are we still following the Law of Moses? Are we followers of Jesus? Or Muhammad? Furthermore, what attributes does this God have? What's He or She like?

The third question is the most emotional. "Am I love?" Many people have given up their faith on this question. They believe that God cannot be good if He allows suffering. So, in their minds, He is either cruel, too far removed to matter, or non-existent. My guess is that you have experienced some suffering in your life, and if so, you will have to come deeply into this question before proceeding.

Am I the King of All

The fourth question, "Am I the King of all?" is the foundation on which the other three questions rest. The foundation of any structure must be the most solid, for it holds up everything else. In our case, with this conversation, we must contemplate that if there is a God, and we know who He is, and we know that He is good…then we should move from self-rule to God-rule. But we must first decide that He is in control, before we can decide if He should be in control of our lives specifically.

Am I
Love
Am I
Who
Am I
Am I the King of All

Question: Am I?

When the original Hebrew Bible was written (the Torah), it was intended for a people who already believed in God. It was written by and for people who had seen the majesty of God displayed; perhaps you are familiar with the Biblical accounts of the exodus from Egypt, the parting of the sea, the pillars of smoke and fire, the thunder on the mountain, the clouds over the tent of meeting, the taking of the Promised Land, and the judgment carried out upon people who disobeyed.

While some people may not have liked the God they experienced, there was no question that they had seen His power. While future generations were unfaithful to God, they were close enough to God's visible presence that many of them still knew what it was like to experience God in a tangible way.

As future scriptures were written, as oral law was passed down, and as written laws were explained, they were delivered to a people who already believed. Their convictions and obedience to their God may have waned, but their belief in Him had not. The existence of God was assumed, and His supernatural presence was taken for granted. Even the enemies of Israel knew that God existed, and they were fearful of Him.

Thus, Old Testament scripture was not written to convince people that God existed. It was created to remind people of what God had done for them. This is why the Old Testament sometimes feels like a history book. The authors were documenting the miracles of God for the people of God. Remembering God and His mighty works was a key element of their faith.

Similarly, New Testament scripture was not written to persuade people that God would send a Messiah; it was written to convince them that the Christ had already come. This is why the New Testament feels more engaging to me than the Old Testament, even while also documenting historical accounts of Jesus.

In both cases, God was understood as a premise of the writing. And God's intention to deliver His people was presumed. To convince people that God existed and that He cared for His people would have felt like a ridiculous waste of time. It would have insulted the intelligence of the people reading or hearing it.

Sadly, this is no longer the case. Many religions today find themselves in the position of not only defending their particular brand of faith, but also the concept of having faith at all. Our culture celebrates celebrity and humanity, tending to honor itself more than it esteems anything outside of itself. While it may pay occasional lip service to a generic God when it is expedient to a moment of crisis or grief, a large segment of the population no longer consciously accepts the premise that I Am…is.

Here we have one of the primary problems modern culture has with religion in general and scripture more specifically. If a society does not believe in or honor God, the very scriptures and sermons that point to Him will not resonate. It's an unfortunate circular logic. Scripture is needed to fix the culture, but the culture has no interest in scripture. The eventual outcome of this downward spiral is not just a rejection of scripture and religion; it is the altogether forgetting of it. To paraphrase T. S. Eliot's "The Hollow Men," our lives of faith may not end with a bang, but a whimper.

Even some who profess Christianity as their religion spend little time in the pursuit of their own faith; so much so that what they hear and read run right through them, making little or no impact on their spirit or their day-to-day lives. One's ability to absorb truth is only as strong or as weak as their belief in the truth.

One's ability to absorb truth is only as strong or as weak as their belief in the truth.

In the earliest part of my return to the Christian faith, believers would want to get me into church and Bible study. I professed Christ, and so they thought the Word of God would be helpful. But in reality, I was hiding behind my religion. Scripture meant nothing to me even though I wanted it to. I read it occasionally because I thought I was supposed to, but every word felt like an academic chore. My time in church was infrequent and insincere. If I did make it into a pew, more time was spent thinking about what I'd have for lunch after the service than what was being served up front for my benefit.

Information was not the problem. There was plenty of that. It was how the information interacted with me that made the difference. It came in, found nothing in me, and went out. For God's power to make a difference, it requires something in us to attach to. It does not require much, but it does require something. Had I only the tiniest belief, my whole perspective would have shifted, and my life would have transformed much earlier, causing less pain to me and my family.

We see this notion play out in the account of Jesus' return to his hometown of Nazareth. His former neighbors saw him only as a child who once played in their streets, a child of Joseph and Mary. They did not view him as God, and as a result, "He did not do many mighty works there because of their unbelief" (Matthew 13:58). They limited God through their unbelief in Him. (See also Psalm 78:41.) This is also what Jesus meant, in part, when he said not to cast pearls before swine (Matthew 7:6). People who don't have any belief will not be able to absorb wisdom and power cast in their direction.

For God's power to make a difference, it requires something in us to attach to.

In most accounts, a miracle of Jesus was either preceded with a question around belief, or a subsequent comment that faith was the reason things worked out so well. It is thus quite instructive that we should look inside our own belief system in order to see Jesus active in our present-day lives. We must return to the most important concept of all, the fact that God…is.

It feels a bit like going back to kindergarten to learn the alphabet, but better to start from scratch than not to start at all. Even Joshua, only one half step removed from Moses, had to convince his people (many of whom had walked through the Red Sea as children) that the living God was among them (Joshua 3:10).

God's first question to you: "Am I?"

It does not require a crisis to lead you out of the middle ground, but it does require time, desire, meditation, prayer, and patience. And as with every journey, it begins with a single step. This is our first step.

To get to the heart of what you really believe about a living God, think of this as a binary question for now. The answer is either *yes* or *no*. God is, or God is not. Assume, only for now, there is no such thing as believing a little. That is simply unbelief dressed up to look like belief.

We can argue later about who God is, what God looks like, how God reveals Himself, how God speaks, or how God feels about us, but all these questions assume there is a God.

Remove all judgment and religious opinion about what you should believe, or what your parents taught you, or what your friends think. Ask God (even if you're not sure God exists) to show you your true heart on this matter. Put the book down, and seriously examine what is inside of you on this question. Take as long as it takes, even if that means days spent away from this reading.

God asks you, "Am I? Do I even exist to you? Am I real?"

Are you ready to continue? What did He say to you, if anything? If so, write it down so you can reflect on it later. I would encourage you to journal throughout your questions.

It is likely that if you answered "no," you felt pretty convicted about it. Even people who are not believers realize what a big decision it is to reject God, if for no other reason than because it may put them at odds with co-workers, friends, and family. Thus, most people who say "no" feel fully confident in their rejection.

If you said "yes," on the other hand, it's possible that your response was much more qualified than the "no" people. You may have gotten to a yes, but you're still not sure what that means. That's okay. It doesn't take much to begin. God will honor your beginning and work with you as long as it takes. I forced you into a yes or no, but the reality is that most people start with very little belief and build from there.

But build we must. The personal implications of our decision are vast. There are two scenarios to consider. The first: If there is no God, nothing matters. Nature rules, or more like it, nothing rules. There is no purpose or order to life. We live for a moment, and then we die. Everyone can do what is right in his or her own eyes. There is no absolute truth, no value system, no judgment, no expectation, and nothing outside of you. Therefore, live for yourself. Put the book down, and go eat, drink, and be merry.

And, the second: If there is a God, everything matters. The entire game changes. Completely. Someone created you. Someone loves you. Someone has hopes for you and expectations of you. Someone is a witness of you, all the time. You belong to someone. There is a reason for the good and bad in your life. There is a plan for things that happen. There is purpose. There is meaning, even in suffering (maybe especially in suffering). You are more than your circumstances.

You are more than your circumstances.

The difference between these two scenarios is so immense one would think it would be life-changing in an extraordinary way. And yet, like many people, I lived most of my life professing that there was a God (scenario 2), but living like there was not (scenario 1). I professed there was an almighty presence in my life, but rarely thought of Him. I confessed He was my Creator, and yet I acted as though my body was my own. I said that He loved me, but spent no time in relationship with Him. I said that Jesus was my Savior, and yet I did not trust and respond to what He did for me or what He said to me. I claimed that He was Lord and yet lived my life under self-rule.

Even though my belief was no more than window dressing, I still wondered why there was no peace or power in my life. I was neither fully in scenario 1 nor in scenario 2. I was in limbo between the two, occasionally moving closer to one or the other depending on my circumstances. I wanted the benefits of each scenario, without the costs of either. I wanted the safety of having God when I needed Him, but the freedom to be in control of my life. I never bought in, was never convicted, never clear. It was time to plant a flag in one camp or the other.

He is simultaneously easy for us to know, and yet so deep we could never begin to fathom His majesty.

It is said that the wisdom of God is a river in which a gnat can swim, and an elephant can drown. He is simultaneously easy for us to know, and yet so deep we could never begin to fathom His majesty. We can approach Him as a novice, and then spend decades trying to understand Him as an expert, but never unraveling His mystery. He meets us where we are, but we will also spend our lives trying to find Him in each precious moment. He is steel, and He is vapor in any given time. He is firmly our foundation, and yet impossible to grasp.

Our journeys of faith will likewise be a bit of a mystery, both simple and complex. There will be flashes of clarity contrasted with moments where we feel lost in a vast ocean. There will be flickers of certainty about His presence, and moments we feel abandoned and unsure. We will search for a formula in the way He moves, but never find one. We will be left, at times, completely perplexed.

In our early walk, this can cause us to vacillate between different levels of faith in a God we cannot see or easily define. There may be times that the best we can do is simply acknowledge there is a God. We may not like Him, we may not trust Him, we may not understand Him, but we know He is there. That is all that is required at this stage. Acknowledgment is the first step. As we mature, belief will be a step beyond acknowledgment, just as faith will be a step beyond belief.

But it is enough for now to have entered into the sphere of acknowledging that God lives, which allows us to read scripture as it was intended—the Word of God for the people of God. It is in this acknowledgment that we receive the invitation that gives us entry into a relationship with the divine, even one that questions and doubts. It is the beginning of our walk, but one that opens up all the benefits of being in the family, even while we still squabble about what is what.

Question: Who Am I?

Although our first question "Am I" is the biggest leap for many people in their faith journey, the "Who am I?" question is the most controversial. For millennia, people have argued over this point, and the responses have been as diverse as the people answering. During the last few thousand years, deities have included nature gods, mythical gods of ancient Greece and Rome, prophets, enlightened humans, humanoids, and the almighty God worshiped by some of the world's largest religions.

Wars have been fought, people have been tortured, and entire towns destroyed or enslaved over which god is which. Families are devastated, and for that matter, nations are divided over this question. Some feel excluded from their community or trapped into believing what others believe for their safety, their livelihood, or family peace. Religion, which was originally intended to be inclusive, has devolved in some cases into exclusion. Even non-believers can be exclusionary, claiming that Christians (or any group of believers) are ignorant and narrow minded.

No belief system can ever be built sustainably through force, coercion, degradation, or violence. It is built through love, patience, and the Spirit of God speaking to us through a variety of thoughts and insights. He draws us in with the right message, at the right time, delivered during the right circumstance. He does not take us by the neck, kicking and screaming into the kingdom. He gently extends His loving embrace, giving us the time and space we need to joyfully accept Him.

By addressing "Who am I?," we call into question God's specificity, His nature, and His history. Is He loving or judgmental? Has He ever walked the Earth? Is He a specific person or being? Did He create us and walk away, or is He involved in the details of our lives? Does He work supernaturally, or did He create the laws of nature and leave us to work it out? These are huge questions that can only be vaguely touched upon with our limited understanding. It is no wonder that we struggle with how to answer such questions and that we develop such a wide variety of ways to worship.

No belief system can ever be built sustainably through force, coercion, degradation, or violence.

Religious studies help frame some of our views, but even there we find factions and disagreement. Christians argue over the one true faith, Muslims argue over which family member or friend of Muhammad to follow, and Jews argue over reform or orthodoxy. All religions debate how we should live, what rules we should follow, and which God or prophet empowered one group over any other.

These are essential topics to address and respectful conversations can be helpful in coming into deeper understanding of our faith and other beliefs. We learn more about our God when we ponder what He expects from us at work, at home, and in our community. We more fully understand Him when we take time to come into relationship with the people around us, and the people from distant nations. The church, at its best, is a wonderful gathering place to help us explore these questions in our community and around the world.

My personal faith was built upon the teachings of the western Christian Church, and I continue to draw much sustenance there. But as I have experienced faith through the eyes of my Christian brothers and sisters in India, China, Europe, the Baltics, Canada, Mexico, and the Middle East, my view of God has both changed and expanded. I have seen other forms of worship, and now have a different, even more positive, view of God the Father, God the Son, and God the Holy Spirit.

I had a similar growth experience during a recent trip to the Holy Land, where the stories of my youth about Jesus were challenged to a degree. While this led me to a temporary period of disorientation, my faith has grown much stronger now that I have a deeper view of who my Savior was and is. I am more "sold out" to Jesus and the God of Abraham, Isaac, and Jacob than I have ever been. I know which God I worship, and He has revealed Himself to me in both natural and supernatural ways over the years. I have plenty of evidence to support my faith, both personally and Biblically.

But this is *my* faith. You must ultimately build your faith. Others can encourage your faith, instruct your faith, model faith for you, and pray about your faith, but it must be built individually and specifically. No one can hand you your faith. You must work out your own salvation (Philippians 2:12). *The intention of this book is not to answer your questions and tell you what to think. It is to ask you questions so you become more conscious of what you already think.* Only when we know what we believe can we become satisfied with where we are, or discover a need and desire to transform.

We can incorrectly assume that faith is based solely on the answers we uncover, when in reality it is built on the questions we ask. Questions imply a seeking heart, which opens us up to God's wisdom. Answers can imply a closed heart, already certain no matter what sits in front of us. Questions imply humility. Answers run the risk of arrogance.

No one can hand you your faith. You must work out your own salvation.

In his book, *Sapiens*, Yuval Harari makes the case that the greatest advancements in human history occurred only after science exhibited a willingness to admit ignorance. The acceptance of the phrase "We do not know," or the Latin conjunction *ignoramus*, launched all manner of scientific breakthroughs. Rather than wallowing in the narrow path of the known world, science launched into the unknown with an entire range of new questions...questions that led to new answers, which led to more questions and so on.

We are where we are today, scientifically, because people were willing to admit ignorance. The same can be true for our journey of faith. Questions will lead us beyond what we've been told in concept and bring us deeper into the specifics of our personal lives. Questions will cause us to contemplate our present condition and clarify what we do and do not believe. That will, in turn, either turn us off entirely, or cause us to step deeper into the wonderful abyss of God's mystery, ever present in your life and mine.

This should not concern us, but rather delight us (James 1:2-3). Once we step into God's will, however superficially at first, our lives become a quest for truth. Each encounter, each meeting, each tragedy or triumph becomes a dialogue with the Almighty. We uncover, moment-by-moment, another piece in the puzzle that is our God…that is our faith. Nothing is what we thought it was, based on our past view of our existence. Every moment becomes alive, ripe with anticipation. Even the trying times offer a window into the nature of our loving Father and an opportunity to come into personal relationship with Him.

Their lives of purpose and meaning began only when they stopped thinking of God as a concept, and instead as a God who saw them personally and specifically.

There are so many stories in the Bible about very strong men and women of faith. They were average people like you and me, but somehow, they stepped into a relationship with God that transformed their lives. Their lives of purpose and meaning began only when they stopped thinking of God as a concept, and instead as a God who saw them personally and specifically.

And so, God asks you "Who am I?"

Pause for a moment. Listen for as long as it takes. Write your thoughts down, and study them before proceeding.

If I were to ask you who your Earthly father is, you might tell me his name, but you would probably also tell me something about him. You might tell me where he lives, or about his career, or whether he was a loving father or a tough one. You might tell me a bit about your mother and siblings, since your father is part of your entire family. You would initially describe him in terms of a noun (father, name), but probably more so later as an adjective (personality, qualities, and characteristics) or a verb, (what he does).

"Who am I" is more than whether you are a Christian or Buddhist (noun). It's about what God means to you and how you think of Him (adjective). It's about how He has spoken into your personal life and the relationship you have with Him. It's about where He lives, distantly in heaven, or up close and personal. It's about how intimate you are as compared to how well you know Him intellectually.

God invites you to the question that asks Him who He is in this moment. Who am I?

Question: Am I Love?

God is Love. Or so says the Apostle John (1 John 4:8). And what could be wrong with that? Who could argue with a God who not only shows love, but also *is* love itself? If God is love, then every time a sentient being feels love, expresses love, receives love, or seeks love, God is present and living through them. He is not only the source of love, He is in the expression of love and in the receiving of it. He completes the circle. It's part of what makes us all "one" as some new-agers like to say. As God moves in and through us as love, we see how we are all connected.

Anyone who has truly experienced what it is to be loved has felt that connection, and also felt something much larger than himself or herself. During a wedding, the birth of a child, or in receiving help during a personal crisis, witnessing or experiencing true love at a deep, personal level is transformative. It is not even necessary to explain that someone who has been loved deeply is a very different person from someone who has never been loved. Profound love changes a person at any level. And so, to enter into relationship with a God who is love offers each of us the opportunity to be transformed any time we turn toward Him.

When Christianity is practiced as Jesus taught it, love is the primary command, the sole requirement, and the only "work" we are to live out in each and every moment. In so doing, we change not only ourselves, but also the communities around us. Even anti-Christian historical records show that the love of Christians positively impacted the societies in which they lived. In today's time, many schools, hospitals, orphanages, and shelters owe both their origin and their current resources to Christians who placed love above all else—including personal wealth, health, and safety.

According to the Bible, love is how we experience God and show that we are a part of His family. Love was the new commandment that Jesus gave to His disciples, which was bold both as a statement and as a philosophy. Until then only Moses could give a commandment from God, and as the years passed, most of the man-made laws that followed were based on quid pro quo—if you give, then I'll give, and if you take, then I'll take. In His command to love one another as He loved us, Jesus was turning the entire Jewish worldview of His day on its head.

Profound love changes a person at any level.

Perhaps that should not be a surprise given that love was part of His life from the beginning. The best-known verse of scripture is John 3:16. "For God so loved the world that he gave his only begotten Son, that whosoever believeth in Him should not perish, but have everlasting life." God expresses His love through giving, and intends for us to experience His love through receiving. For in receiving God's love we will not only fill our own need, but we will overflow with love onto those around us. It's a virtuous circle that many of us experience in the closest personal relationships we hold dear.

Today I played with my grandson for most of the day. The more we played, the more spontaneously he said to me, "I love you." And each time he said it, I fell more deeply in love with him and the more I wanted to give him the experience of joy. And the more I engaged with him, the more he kept saying, "I love you." Not once did I give him anything material. It was in the simple act of play and caring for each other that our encounter of love kept growing. We just kept giving to each other. It was the sheer excitement of being together that caused his spontaneous feelings of deep connection.

This is the relationship God calls for us to have with Him. He wants to show us love, and He wants us to love Him back; not because He needs it, but because the act of loving Him generates more love in us and a deeper connection with Him. When we love Him just for whom He is and not for what we think He should be, our trust and awareness of whom He truly is increases.

As that back and forth flow continues over time, the grander it becomes in our awareness and in our experience. My grandson did not immediately love me this way the first day we met. It was the constant cultivation of the relationship over time that caused us to be so totally in synch and to know we have each other's back even when the trouble comes.

Yet, as much as I love my grandson, it could never compare to the love my Father has for him. Nor would His love always be expressed in the same way that I think it should be. For as heaven is higher than the Earth, God's ways are different than our ways (Isaiah 55:9). As much as I want to pour out my love to my family, God would express it differently, deliver it differently, and time it differently than I would. In other words, my definition of love is not always the same as God's. For all I know, it is never the same.

And this difference in the definition of love is where the world steps in and somehow manages to distort the notion that God is love. Those with no belief or weak faith see only the circumstances of what the world is like, or what their marriage is like, or what their health is like, or what the state of destructive politics is like. They see only the present and only the struggle. And since it doesn't suit their needs or their liking, they cannot come to grips with the thought that God is love.

Our faith has evolved into a WIIFM faith—what's in it for me? If things are "good" for me, then God is love. But if things are "bad" for me, then God is not love. And only I get to define what is good and what is bad, and only I am allowed to determine the timing of good things, the method as to how good things happen, and the amount of work I have to put in to achieve the good things. This is a formula for disappointment and an assurance that I will conclude that God is not love.

This was my perspective for much of my adult life. Times were tough, and I thought I had only three options to choose from. The first was that God did not exist. The second was that I was bad and was deserving of bad things. The third was that God is cruel, capricious, and merciless.

But over time, the possibility of another option kept brewing in the back of my mind. As I looked at my two-year-old child suffering, I could not imagine that God would punish her for my sins. Nor could I contemplate a God who would allow a child to suffer for any reason at all. And yet, for some reason, I knew there was a God.

Am I love?

This question, "Am I love?" has a corollary question, "Am I to be trusted?" For if God is not love, nor is He a God with good intentions, what faith can I have in Him? And if God is not in control, what faith can I have in Him? I can only have unencumbered faith in a God I completely trust, and trust is built upon His ability to control the outcome, and control it for my eventual good. Otherwise, I can hope for the best and plan for the worst with God, but I will not trust Him. And if I don't trust Him, I cannot love Him with all my being.

. . . if I don't trust Him, I cannot love Him with all my being.

Human love has expectations. It expects that the other party involved in the loving relationship will be a constant source for meeting our expectations, which never works out entirely. We do not love perfectly, and so we bring an imperfect definition of love to the God who created it. We extrapolate our view of love onto God and judge His loving based upon an imperfect definition, which is "Do we get what we want from God?" And so, we neither love nor trust because no one gets everything he wants from God.

But our question here is not "Do we love God?" It is more "Does God love us?" Since we are human, we will bring more than a bit of skepticism to this question based on our experiences in life. God, it seems, lets us down continually. We carry this baggage into our one-sided relationship, and we question His motives, His results, and His consistency. Since we experience suffering in our lives, then we can't trust God, nor can He possibly be love.

In his book, *When Bad Things Happen to Good People*, Rabbi Harold S. Kushner makes the argument that God is still perfect and loving, even when bad things happen. He postulates that bad things are the result of disorder, which is not part of God's original creation.

"Nature," he says, "is morally blind, without values. It churns along, following its own laws, not caring who or what gets in the way. But God is not morally blind. I could not worship Him if I thought He was."

Rabbi Kushner believes that God's heart is just as broken as ours when disaster comes and that the love of God is shown *after* nature does its damage. Love is shown and experienced by the people who respond to the earthquake, or the illness, or the tragic accident. It is in this suffering that people are able to experience the love of God—a love they would not have otherwise felt if the suffering did not exist in the first place.

Conversely, in his book, *Trusting God*, Jerry Bridges makes the argument that God is in complete control of life's circumstances, and he calls upon a great deal of scripture to make his point. It is loving control, he argues, but control nonetheless:

> Confidence in the sovereignty (strength, power, rule) of God in all that affects us is crucial to our trusting Him. If there is a single event in all of the universe that can occur outside of God's sovereign control, then we cannot trust Him. His love may be infinite, but if His power is limited and His purpose can be thwarted, we cannot trust Him. You may entrust to me your most valuable possessions. I may love you, and my aim to honor your trust may be sincere, but if I do not have the power or ability to

guard your valuables, you cannot truly entrust them to me.

Both based on scripture, these views couldn't be more different. And, even though well thought out, neither argument is helpful to those whose hurting souls are in the midst of suffering. Theology can indeed explain how God can be love during difficult times, but only to people who value theology, and only *before* the crisis comes. For in the midst of crisis, all we can see is the crisis, and no amount of words or ideas will console us or prove to us that this has to be for our good.

It is because of suffering that I would suggest this question of "Am I Love?" is the main reason why people leave their faith, and the main reason that so much anti-faith exists in the world. Some people see the world only as it appears, and there is no comfort or faith to be found there. In the heat of suffering, if all we see is our circumstances, it will be an empty place, devoid of God, and inspiring of anti-God sentiments.

How could a loving God allow the world to have slavery, illness, violence, terrorism, natural disasters, accidents, or divorce? It is a complex question that cannot be reasoned simply through the mind, through our emotions, or through an intellectual argument. Every point of pain will work against our faith, either abruptly or cumulatively. The ills of the world will corrode even the strongest of faiths, as wave after wave of tribulation comes.

We can be quick to judge God for His actions and seeming moral failures without spending an equal amount of time trying to understand how God might define His love for us in the context of our lives, let alone eternity. We are not all that different from a child who cannot understand that our studies need to take priority over television so that our lives might be full and free in the future. There is work to be done if we are to realize our full potential and God's specific plan for us.

The apostle Paul wrote half of the New Testament, but he spent most of his Christian life in peril. He was frequently beaten, stoned, tortured, imprisoned, shipwrecked, snake bitten, and abandoned by friends. Yet he wrote continuously about his joy, and he is known for writing one of the most beautiful descriptions of love ever expressed (1 Corinthians 13).

If there were anyone who could claim that God was out to get him, it was Paul. And yet that was not his perspective nor was it his experience. Once he turned his life over to Jesus, Paul's entire life goal was to live his life in the light of the teachings of Christ Jesus, to be more like Him, to bring others to Him, and to establish a faith system that countered everything previously known to humankind. And, as Christ suffered, Paul's goal to be like Christ called for him to suffer as well.

In light of His goal, Paul got exactly what he prayed for. What looks bad to us was very good to him. I am a believer today, in part, because I saw how Jesus transformed Paul's life. Paul went from being militantly anti-Christian to risking everything to show people who Jesus is. He suffered greatly so that I might know Him. Paul has shown me love even though we lived in different millennia.

Am I love?

At one point in my life, I expressed to a friend that I wanted to go into ministry. He laughed and said, "No, you don't." I was a bit taken aback and said that I did indeed want to get into ministry.

He laughed again and said the same thing. I looked at him with conviction and said, "Yes, I do!" His smile faded, and he became more serious. "Scott," he said, "if you want to get into ministry, forces will come against you that you cannot even comprehend. And furthermore, Christ will bring you into His suffering, and you are not ready for that."

Theology can indeed explain how God can be love during difficult times, but only to people who value theology, and only before the crisis comes.

He was right, of course, but I did not think so at the time. Days later as I reflected on his comment, I came to the disappointing conclusion that I didn't want the suffering life. I wanted comfort and peace and, more sadly, a casual relationship with my Lord that would not require me to take up my cross. It was a low point for me. I no longer was defaulting to comfort without thinking about it. I was choosing comfort deliberately over a closer relationship with the being I claimed to worship. I wasn't lukewarm anymore. I had chosen a side, and it was not the right one.

Thanks be to God, He continued to pursue me, and I have now chosen what I believe to be the right side of things. We have developed a relationship where He speaks to me in a variety of ways in order to draw me closer to Him. And indeed, some of that path includes suffering in big ways and small. At times that suffering looks like a 30-year struggle to save a child. In other ways, it is a much less drastic form of suffering that still gets my attention.

Knowing God…who He is and how He loves is often a

counterintuitive process. But then again, so was the entire ministry of Jesus. Almost everything Jesus said demonstrated that God's thoughts are different than ours, God's love is different than ours, God's economy is different than ours, and God's priorities are different than ours. And so, our view of whether or not God is love might require that we turn our entire belief system on its head. It may be that if we truly seek a deeper understanding of God and His love for us that nothing is left of what we once believed, or the way we believed it.

Am I love?

I can remember being in a small group once while we were sharing prayer requests. I had come to a point in my life where I didn't ask for prayer because it would take too long to explain what I needed, and at that point in my journey, I didn't feel like any of the prayers were actually working. But this particular group kept pressing me, and so I finally relented. By the time my prayer request was described, the entire room went silent, which is another reason I stopped asking. Whenever I let people in on what we were living, it always seemed to overwhelm everyone else's prayer needs.

But to this day, I remember the prayer leader and what he said to me. "Scott, if I were God, I would handle your problems very differently. I'd take all of this pain away for you and your entire family. But I'm not God, and you should be thankful that I'm not." The leader of our group could not explain, nor did he try to explain our pain. He didn't try to answer complex theological questions about whether God caused the pain, allowed the pain, or simply grieved over the pain. He just came alongside me.

Today I can look back on my life with joy, because I now

live *in* joy, even though some of these same issues still press in on the family and me. But I can say without question that I would not be a disciple of Christ today if my life had gone smoothly. I would not know God the way I know Him today. I would not have a relationship with Him. I would still be firmly in the middle, neither hot nor cold. I'd still profess my faith but have no substance to it. And I can't think of a more loving thing for God to have done for me than to change everything I knew, everything I believed, and everything I trusted. He undid me, and then recreated me. That, to me, is love beyond any human understanding.

He didn't try to answer complex theological questions about whether God caused the pain, allowed the pain, or simply grieved over the pain. He just came alongside me.

Thus, our answer to "Am I love?" will rely on many things. Not only will it be grounded on our personal experience, but it will also be built on our interpretation of these experiences. It will be constructed on whether we predominantly see the bad or the good in life. It will be established on our view of how love is demonstrated across a wide variety of circumstances. It will be centered on how tuned in we are to how God speaks to us individually. It will depend on what we are praying for. It will be based on how deeply we want to know Him and how much we may need to endure to truly understand who He is. It will be founded on whether we think God created the world and stepped away, or whether He is involved in the minute details of daily life.

So, God invites you into a conversation that may have more layers than the other questions we have asked ourselves. It may have more nuances and more complexity as you try to compare your life experience to what scripture says about God as love.

Am I love? Can you see it now?

Pause, reflect, and journal.

Question: Am I the King of All?

God is great, God is good, God we thank you for this food.

This child's prayer is so simple, and yet it captures everything we need to know about God. He is great; all-powerful, all knowing, totally in control, and our King. And He is good. He is a benevolent ruler, and our response to that is gratitude. One could argue that this is virtually all we need to know to both start and fulfill our lives of faith. When we (finally) agree with, submit to, value, and feel gratitude for God's rule over our lives, God's greatest plan *for* us can begin its journey *in* us.

And yet God's power is such an alien idea that most do not even contemplate the notion, let alone submit to it. Even some who consider themselves religious do not reflect upon God's rule in their specific personal lives, even while giving Him credit for creating and ruling the world in general. They would fight to the death to protect His name, but also push back or ignore Him from having a say in where they work, where they live, how they raise their children, and who they are called to serve.

The story of Jonah is a great visual for this topic. When told to go to Nineveh and warn his enemies of God's pending wrath, Jonah traveled hundreds of miles in the opposite direction, putting him and others in peril. After being thrown into the sea by his shipmates, he was said to have been swallowed by a big fish. It was not until he was vomited up onto the shore of the country he was directed to serve in the first place that Jonah finally came to understand that God was in control; not only of the wind and the sea, but over him specifically.

The path to accepting God's authority in our lives is often a messy road. Jonah's greatest revelation came while covered in fish bile and seaweed. The same is often true, albeit more figuratively, of ourselves. We fight His direction so consistently and fervently that the path to acceptance often requires something drastic to get our attention. Jonah needed a big fish and a tough few days. I needed to be worn down over decades.

The path to accepting God's authority in our lives is often a messy road.

But when people finally see God's majesty, they are overwhelmed and overcome with the notion of just how majestic He is. Even those who saw God in the flesh still could not grasp what God was like in the Spirit. God's majesty is more than we can comprehend, let alone absorb. It is humbling news to those who think they are in control and encouraging news to those who know they are not. Regardless of how we get there, we must come to a point where we cede control to a mighty sovereign.

If our first three questions from God were building blocks, this last question is the foundation upon which we place them; for our answer butts up against the most destructive force of our human nature—the desire to be our own god. Our willingness to submit entirely to an all-powerful God is at the core of our obedience, or lack thereof, and it is at the heart of our ability to hear and follow God's voice. This revelation can be the turning point in a life of faith or, if we reject it, can be at the center of our backsliding and disappointment.

The question over God's power is *the* question that determines the extent of our belief and the effectiveness of our faith. If I do not believe that God is in complete control, there is no way that I can believe entirely that He can deliver what I need in any specific moment. If I think He is randomly in control or capricious in His benevolence, He is not a God to be trusted. And if I do not trust Him, I can have no faith in His ability or willingness to be the ruler of my life. I still might ask for His help, but I can't really, sincerely, expect an answer.

Therefore, our response to whether God is in control—completely in control—is either the bedrock on which we build our faith, or it is the rock over which we stumble and scatter (Matthew 21:44). It is the issue that causes the rising and falling of many (Luke 2:34). It is the subject that will set us on fire *for* God, or just set us on fire.

This is not to say that things will be easy in a life of obedience to our benevolent ruler. Jesus obeyed and was crucified. The apostles obeyed and were put to death in horrible ways. Yet even as faithful men and women have gone to their demise, they have done so more fulfilled and on purpose than at any point in their lives. We are fulfilled when God is sovereign. We are of greatest use when God is sovereign. We have peace, even in the midst of turmoil, when God is sovereign.

Am I the King of all? Am I *your* King?

As with all our questions, I invite you to pause, pray, and journal before proceeding.

Whether you believe in the creation account found in Genesis or not, the story (or allegory) of Adam and Eve is nonetheless instructive. Their sin was not so much that they ate the fruit; it was much more their desire to be like God and live apart from His rule. It was the temptation to be something God never intended us to be—separate from Him, on our own, with our own plans. All our pain, all our suffering, and all our sins have come from this one destructive desire for self-rule apart from the God who created us.

In my own journey, I can trace every good or bad thing to this one issue. My worst outcomes came from my own pride and self-assurance. My greatest victories came from surrender. Good consequences came from submission; bad consequences came from my own making. A compassionate heart came from looking to my Savior for every next step. An angry, vengeful, and bitter heart came from my striving and planning.

This was Paul's struggle, the battle that raged within him as described in Romans 7. Who would he allow to rule his life as each and every moment unfolded, his Lord or the ever-present desire to be lord? The reality is that someone is always sovereign in your life. The only question is, is it you, God, or an idol of some kind?

Like most, I struggle with Paul's internal battle. I want to do good works, but I don't. I want to be kind, but I'm not. I want to be selfless, but instead I am selfish. And I know the problem. If you asked me to describe myself, I would eventually get around to saying that I am fiercely independent. I am anti-authority. I feel completely constrained around structure and rules. I want to control my own destiny.

And yet, this is not how I should live my life. I am stronger when I am helped. I am nicer when I am connected to other people. I see better ways to do things when I reach out for advice. I am more compassionate when I see others serve in ways that I don't see intuitively on my own. I am more successful in a secular world when I marshal smart people together to find the best way to solve problems.

But I rebel anyway. I think I can get there faster on my own, better on my own, and more profitably on my own. Some of that is just me; it's who I am. It's my personality. But a lot of it is also what I inherited from Adam. It's human nature, no matter how obvious that nature may appear in some people, or how subtle it may express itself in others. We fight for independence. We reward independence, and we celebrate those who pull themselves up by their bootstraps. We make movies about people who have done it all on their own, and we strive to be like them.

The reality is that someone is always sovereign in your life. The only question is, is it you, God, or an idol of some kind?

We want to play God at best, and we want to replace God at worst. So, it should be no surprise that this fourth question regarding God's power is the most difficult of the faith questions we have asked so far. It's both the hardest to identify as a problem, and it's the most stubborn to put right. It is, after all, Sin with a capital S. It's the "biggie" question. It is how we walk into God's plans, or how we, like Jonah, seek to escape them and plot our own path, no matter how destructive it may be.

So, what of our friend Jonah? When Jonah finally arrived in

Nineveh, the entire population repented of its sin and returned to a life subservient to God. The Almighty had been doing a work in them for years, and it only took a few words from Jonah for them to understand what was in store if they continued their rebellion. God wanted someone to speak His truth. It was a simple truth that had profound impact on an entire community.

We want to play God at best, and we want to replace God at worst.

In an ironic twist, the story of Jonah ends in a lonely place. Jonah overlooked the city and people he just saved and regretted their repentance. These people were his enemy, and he lamented the gift of salvation God had bestowed upon them. Jonah was grateful for the grace God had bestowed upon him, but he resented the grace God gave to his enemies. In the end, his last request to God was that he should die rather than see God's love poured out on people Jonah deemed less worthy. In other words, he questioned God's judgment about his own life, and he questioned God's wisdom as to whom He would show favor.

As with Jonah, Adam lives in the heart of us all, even those who have experienced God's majesty first-hand. Our rebellion to this authority causes us much misery. We scheme, we plan, and we regret our many willful actions. Some would rather that God kill them than bear their misery any longer. We wonder how a loving God could allow such terrible things to happen. We wonder why God doesn't speak to us. We wonder why life is so hard.

We've done it to ourselves.

Our journey of faith must determine whether or not we believe in God's ultimate power and strength. Life will have its moments of uncertainty regardless of our answer, *but how we think will shape our view on whether we see the big fish as a reprimand or a rescue.* If we see it as a reprimand, our view of God will be one of judgment and unpredictability. If we see it as a rescue, we will glory in His majesty and the way He orchestrates miracles to achieve His purposes. One view detracts from faith; the other builds faith.

So, God invites you into a conversation to accept Him as Lord. **Am I the King over your life specifically?**

Final Thoughts

Peter is often thought of as an impetuous disciple; quick to respond, quick to lash out, and quick to rush into situations of all kinds for both better and worse. But he is perhaps best known to most Christians as the one who denied Jesus three times. This man, who was part of the inner circle of three (James and John being the other two), denied his Lord at the time He needed him most. Not only that, but Jesus predicted he would do so, even despite Peter boasting he would stand by Jesus to the end as the only faithful follower of the group.

We can only imagine the shame, grief, and disgust Peter must have felt in himself when Jesus looked across the courtyard and gazed into Peter's eyes after the third denial (Luke 22:61). We read only that Peter wept and ran, but we can easily envision how painful the next several days must have been for him. We can also imagine the joy he would have felt when he heard that his Lord had risen, but also perhaps the nervous anticipation of what life with Jesus after the courtyard denials would look like.

While Peter may have been anxious about seeing the resurrected Jesus, he should not have been. Jesus is a loving encourager and would have found a way to replace Peter's shame with the love of God. On the day He chose to restore Peter, Jesus approached His friends from afar, standing on the shore seemingly as a stranger. He called out to the boat where the disciples had been fishing and repeated the exact miracle He performed on the day He first called Peter into His ministry three years earlier.

For the second time in this same miracle, the disciples lowered their nets on His command and pulled in more fish than they could possibly handle. For Peter, it had to be an instant reminder of his first encounter. Jesus was calling him into ministry once again. Peter leapt from the boat into the water fully clothed. One could think of this as a baptism of sorts. Peter would not make the same mistake of running away again. This time he would run toward his Lord. He had learned from his weakness and would become a far more influential apostle as a result.

Jesus gave Peter three opportunities to express his love for Him, overcoming the three denials in the courtyard. Peter was reminded how his Lord had pulled him out of his sinful life and gave him a new name, new life, and new spirit. By the time they left the beach that day, Peter would no longer be the disciple who denied Jesus. His Holy-Spirit-given faith in Jesus as Messiah would finally take on the mantel as the rock on which Jesus would build His church.

And yet, despite these amazing revelations, Peter still didn't get it completely. Rather than basking in the love and forgiveness that was just afforded to him by Jesus, Peter took his eyes off his Lord and asked about John's fate. (For whatever reason, Peter seemed to have an issue with John.) After receiving this incredible gift of restoration and forgiveness, he reverted to the old Peter and asked Jesus "But Lord, what about this man?" Jesus replied, "…what's it to you? You follow Me." (John 21:22)

The essence of His message was, "Don't worry about anyone else's walk with Me. Just focus on your own walk with Me." And that is perhaps the key message of this book as well. Don't put your faith in your faith, your church, your denomination, or your friends. You have your own path to walk toward your Savior, and that is what you should focus on first and foremost.

Your personal, unique walk with Jesus will then determine how you interact with the world, not the other way around. Your own personal walk will determine how you add value to the church, and whom you will call to the church.

Before you can be a help to others, you must first walk your specific path...fully, deeply, and completely. That walk will be in community with others, and yet it will be abundantly personal and specific to you. He is calling you to come out of the desert and into a vibrant relationship with Himself. He is calling you to choose, to believe, to trust, and to act. He is looking for you to come into awareness of who you are, who He is, and how He wants you to live out your greatest self.

Your path will not be comfortable. No quest ever is. God does not lead us into our comfort, He leads us into His glory. Yet, when we see this path as the road to the treasure of our own faith-life, the difficulties become more adventure than suffering. We come to rejoice in our sufferings because it helps us to know Him more deeply and intimately.

Our lives of faith do not center on a doctrine or our circumstance. They center on a Person. You can ignore a doctrine or principle. It is far more difficult to ignore a person. And so, we focus on the person of Jesus and our relationship to Him and with Him. When we fall more deeply in love, love cannot help but flow out from us to the rest of the world. And this love will become the evidence of our faith, even while His love is the foundation of our faith.

Jesus becomes the God of our life specifically, not generally. We do not have faith in something out there, somewhere else in our community. We have lives of faith "in here," inside us, marinating in our spirits, acutely aware of God in every person we meet and every circumstance we encounter. We have an awareness of God that we never had before, and a relationship that forms the basis of trust.

Our faith is a choice, at least at first. We must choose to believe as an introductory step. As we take those first steps of faith, walking the unsteady bridge toward our salvation, we gain confidence and begin to walk. The nearer we get, the more anticipation we have, and before we will know it, we are running.

We must leave the safety of our middle ground and leap into our faith, becoming more of what God called us to be. We welcome the messy details, as each step gives us more faith in Him. We run toward Him, just as Peter leapt out of the boat, running toward his resurrected Lord. Can you imagine the joy of having Him restore us, just as Jesus did on the beach that day for Peter?

We can, of course, choose to stay in the boat, or never even get into the boat in the first place. That may indeed mean more comfort for us while in our bodies. On that miraculous morning on the beach, how many people missed out simply because they stayed in their proverbial beds, never having ventured into relationship with the Lord, and never having experienced all the joy and sacrifice it meant to follow Him? But we are not talking about those people today. They are long forgotten.

Our choices impact the legacy we leave and the impact we make on the world. We can choose to see the negative, the logical, the intellectual side of every circumstance, and in the process ignore or disparage even the possibility of something greater than ourselves. That, to me, feels like an empty and unfulfilling place.

One of the most hopeful and instructive parts of the Bible

is found in 1 Corinthians 2:9. From the New Living Translation, "No eye has seen, no ear has heard, and no mind has imagined what God has prepared for those who love Him…But the people who aren't spiritual can't receive the truths from God's Spirit. It all sounds foolish to them and they can't understand it…"

God has already prepared for you more than you could ever dream or accomplish on your own. The Amplified Bible says that He has made and keeps our gifts ready for us. But this abundant life is for those who love Him and have spiritual discernment. What the world cannot even understand, you can experience to the full. Our lives can be lived to their greatest potential. These things are already prepared for you. You only need to take the leap and claim them.

So, tell me…Am I?

A Deeper Look

If you enjoyed this book and want to go deeper, there is a longer version that also explores how to live our faith in day-to-day life. Look for my work, *Am I…Building a Life of Personal Faith*. You can also join us at our website *awarenessofgod.org*, or on all social media channels.

We encourage you to go deeper and invite your friends into the conversation.

About the Author

As an author, international speaker on faith, and entrepreneur, Scott MacLellan, for four decades, has been making an impact in multiple organizations. His focus falls especially on those associations whose mission is to help the impoverished, the addicted, or those who struggle with illness. When not speaking on one of these subjects, he can be found working with a very skilled team of business leaders, or on the coast of South Carolina where he shares his home with his wife of 34 years and his amazing seven-year-old grandson. He has two grown daughters who live in Ohio and South Carolina respectively. More grandchildren are on the way.